Scruffy the Hero

Margaret Clyne
Illustrated by Andrew McLean

CELEBRATION PRESS
Pearson Learning Group

Smithy lived with his grandfather, Captain Curnow, in a stone cottage not far from the harbor. The cottage stood on a small hill.

From the hill, Smithy could see the road winding down to the harbor and his grandfather's fishing boat, *The Crail*, bobbing on the water.

Around the bay, they could see the big red and white lighthouse sitting at the edge of the rocks.

Each evening, as dusk fell, the lighthouse would guide Captain Curnow's fishing boat safely home.

Every morning, Smithy would walk down the hill with his grandfather. He would run down the steps and stand by the pier to watch Captain Curnow set off for the day.

There were lots of little boats in the bay, but *The Crail* was the one that brought back the fish for the people of the village.

One morning when Captain Curnow had just gone aboard, Smithy saw something splashing and struggling in the water. He ran down the steps and yelled out, "Grandfather! Grandfather!"

The Captain leaned over the edge of his boat and hauled the struggling thing out of the water. It was a dog! He was a terrible-looking sight, ears flat, tail down, fur matted and dripping. He was shivering and shaking with cold and fright.

"I better take you home, Pal, and get you cleaned up. You look like a drowned rat. You're lucky to be alive, I'd say," boomed the Captain.

"A bit scruffy, isn't he?" said Smithy.

"Yes he is," laughed the Captain. "We'll call him Scruffy."

So they took Scruffy home and bathed, brushed and fed him. Scruffy ate two bowls of fish pieces and lapped up a full bowl of water. Then he curled up and slept on the rug in front of the fire.

Smithy watched as the warmth of the fire made the steam rise from his coat. He patted him and whispered, "Don't worry Scruffy, you're safe now."

"Can we keep him?" Smithy asked.

"He might belong to someone. I'll tell you what we'll do. We'll put up a big sign outside the cottage and we'll see if anyone comes for him," said the Captain.

The next day, Smithy found a board and some chalk and wrote in his best handwriting:

FOUND

One scruffy dog,

now called "Scruffy."

Inquire inside.

The days passed. Scruffy grew stronger and became less scruffy, but no one came to claim him.

"Not so scruffy now, are you?" the Captain said, as he scratched the top of Scruffy's head.

Scruffy did everything that all dogs do. He wagged his tail, he played with a ball, and he enjoyed long walks. Most of all, Scruffy loved running along the edge of the water and fetching sticks that Smithy would throw.

But there was one thing Scruffy never did— Scruffy never barked.

If a stranger approached, he would stop and stand still like a stone, and the hairs on his back would stand up straight. If he wanted attention, he would paw gently at the Captain or Smithy until he got their attention. But he never barked.

Early each morning, Scruffy would go into the Captain's room and put his paws up on the Captain's shoulder to wake him up.

When the Captain was ready to start his day, he, Smithy and Scruffy would walk down to the pier together.

Later, Smithy would go off to school. When he came home, he would run down to the harbor and wait for *The Crail* to return. He would sit and think about the day when he would be old enough to go out on the boat.

The Captain would say he must "go to school first." Smithy would say how well he knew the tides, how he knew every part of the boat, how he could mend nets, and how he could help to unload the catch.

"That's the truth," the Captain would reply, "You'll make a good captain one day. Just have patience, Smithy. You'll grow up fast enough."

One day Smithy came home from school, changed his clothes, and ran to the pier to wait for *The Crail* to come in. He sat in his usual spot and waited. He waited and he waited until the sun went down. Then he went to see Smiley, who was the Captain's best friend.

Smiley took a lantern and knocked on all the neighbors' doors to tell people that *The Crail* had not returned. He asked people to fetch their lanterns, and come down to the harbor. There they waited and waited, but still there was no sign of the Captain's fishing boat. They sat with their lanterns, looking out to sea.

The night grew colder and everyone was hoping Captain Curnow's boat would appear. The crescent moon did not give much light, but they could see the lighthouse winking in the darkness. Smithy thought the friendly sea now looked dark and frightening. Everything was quiet except for the lapping of the waves on the shore.

Suddenly there was a very faint sound. Everyone sat up and listened carefully. They heard the sound again. Smithy stood up. "It's Scruffy!" he shouted. "It's Scruffy! Scruffy's barking!"

The men moved quickly into the boats and started rowing toward the sound of the barking.

Smithy jumped into the first boat with Smiley. He stood, leaning forward, hoping the barking would not stop.

Suddenly, they all cheered as their lanterns showed the words *The Crail*, and Smithy saw with relief that they had reached the Captain's drifting boat.

Captain Curnow was sitting on the deck, leaning against the mast. "Don't look so worried Smithy," the Captain said, but his voice was weak. "Takes more than a knock to finish off this sailor."

The Captain told everyone how he had tripped over a rope, twisted his ankle badly, and hit his head. He was unable to get up. While *The Crail* drifted on in the dark, Scruffy started barking. He didn't stop barking until the boats arrived.

"You're a hero, Scruffy," said Smithy. Everyone cheered and Scruffy wagged his tail.

When they got back to their cottage, Scruffy was given the largest fish in the day's catch.

"Well," said the Captain with a twinkle in his eye. "I'm going to need someone to help on the boat until I'm better. How about it Smithy? Between you and Scruffy, I'm sure you can keep me out of trouble."

"Did you hear that Scruffy? Did you hear that?" said Smithy, cartwheeling around the cottage.

Scruffy stood and watched him—ears perked up, tail wagging. The little dog didn't bark, and we are told he never had to bark again.